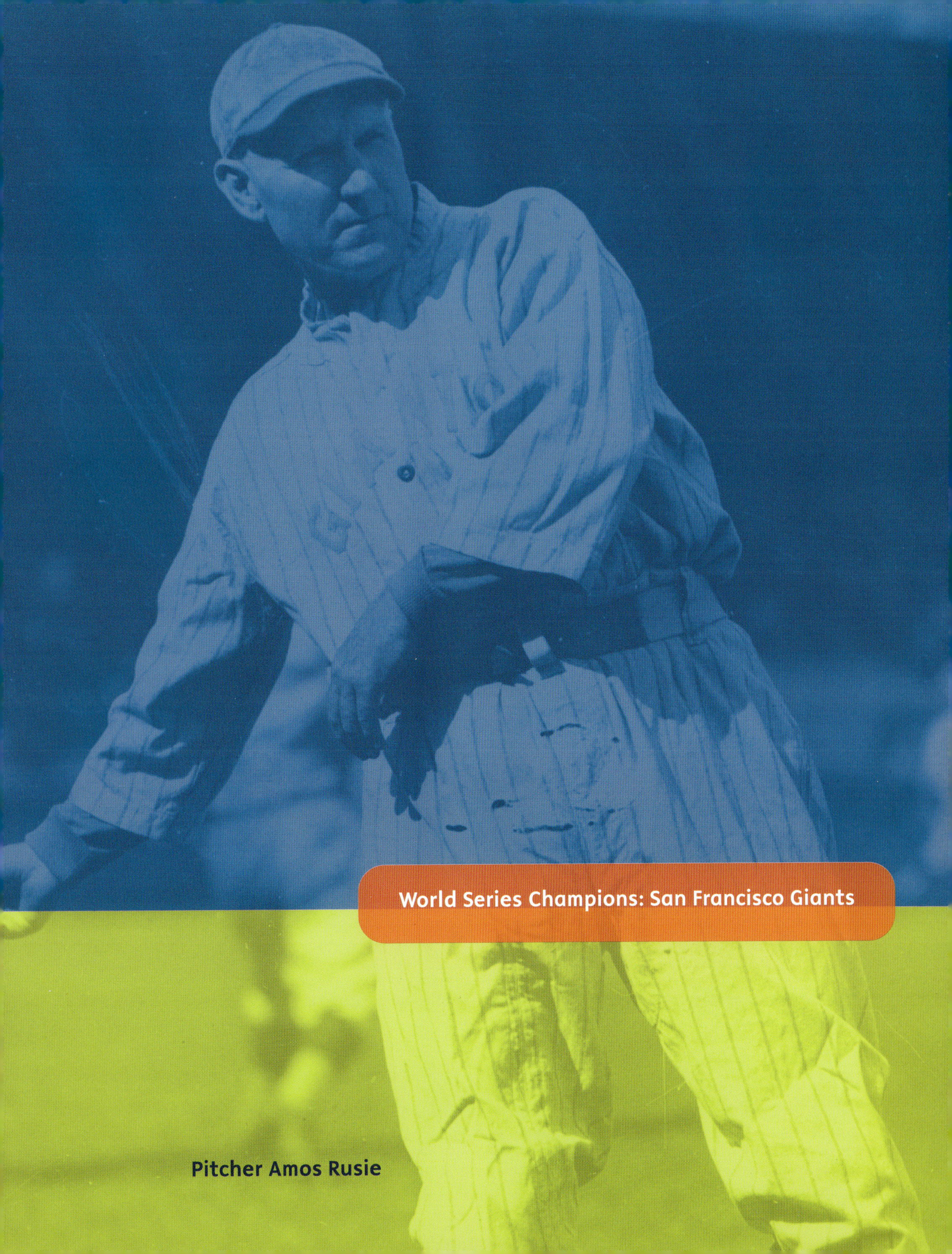

World Series Champions: San Francisco Giants

Pitcher Amos Rusie

Outfielder Barry Bonds

WORLD SERIES CHAMPIONS

SAN FRANCISCO GIANTS

MEGAN COOLEY PETERSON

CREATIVE SPORTS

CREATIVE EDUCATION / CREATIVE PAPERBACKS

Published by Creative Education and Creative Paperbacks
P.O. Box 227, Mankato, Minnesota 56002
Creative Education and Creative Paperbacks are imprints of
The Creative Company
www.thecreativecompany.us

Art Direction by Tom Morgan
Book production by Ciara Beitlich
Edited by Joe Tischler

Photographs by AP Images (David J. Griffin/Icon Sportswire), Corbis (Library of Congress, Robert Riger, Don Smith), Getty (Focus on Sport, Thearon W. Henderson, Brad Mangin, Sacramento Bee, Jamie Squire, Sarah Stier, Transcendental Graphics), iStock (muddymari)

Library of Congress Cataloging-in-Publication Data
Names: Peterson, Megan Cooley, author.
Title: San Francisco Giants / Megan Cooley Peterson.
Description: Mankato, MN : Creative Education and Creative Paperbacks, 2024. | Series: Creative sports. World Series champions | Includes index. | Audience: Ages 7-10 | Audience: Grades 2-3 | Summary: "Elementary-level text and engaging sports photos highlight the San Francisco Giants' MLB World Series wins and losses, plus sensational players associated with the professional baseball team such as Barry Bonds."-- Provided by publisher.
Identifiers: LCCN 2023008205 (print) | LCCN 2023008206 (ebook) | ISBN 9781640268340 (library binding) | ISBN 9781682773840 (paperback) | ISBN 9781640269873 (pdf)
Subjects: LCSH: San Francisco Giants (Baseball team)--History--Juvenile literature. | World Series (Baseball)--History--Juvenile literature.
Classification: LCC GV875.S34 P53 2024 (print) | LCC GV875.S34 (ebook) | DDC 796.357/640979461--dc23/eng/20230330
LC record available at https://lccn.loc.gov/2023008205
LC ebook record available at https://lccn.loc.gov/2023008206

Printed in China

2014 World Series Champions

Pitcher Tim Lincecum

CONTENTS

Home of the Giants

San Francisco is a hilly city in northern California. It is known for the famous Golden Gate Bridge. The city is also home to the Giants baseball team. The Giants have played at a **stadium** called Oracle Park since 2000.

The San Francisco Giants are a Major League Baseball (MLB) team. The Giants play in the National League (NL) West Division. Their **rivals** are the Los Angeles Dodgers. All teams try to win the World Series to become champions. The Giants have won it eight times!

Pitcher Christy Mathewson

Naming the Giants

The Giants started playing as the New York Gothams. In 1885, the team had a huge win. Manager Jim Mutrie was proud of his team. He called them "My big fellows! My giants!" A sportswriter started calling them the Giants. The name stuck.

Second baseman Larry Doyle

Giants History

The Giants played in their first World Series in 1905. They beat the Philadelphia Athletics. Over the next 19 years, the Giants reached eight World Series. Pitcher Christy Mathewson struck out batters. Larry Doyle drove in runs. The Giants won the **title** in 1921 and 1922. They beat the New York Yankees both times.

The Giants added two more World Series titles in New York. Then, in 1958, the team moved to San Francisco. Fans loved them. The Giants reached the World Series in 1962, 1989, and 2002. But they lost every time.

The Giants won their first championship in San Francisco in 2010. They beat the Texas Rangers. Catcher Buster Posey's strong hitting and arm helped his team win. Two years later, Posey and the Giants won again.

Catcher Buster Posey

Pitcher Madison Bumgarner

The Giants beat the Kansas City Royals in the 2014 World Series. Madison Bumgarner pitched a **shutout** in Game 5. It was the third championship for the Giants in five years!

Other Giants Stars

Many star pitchers have worn a Giants uniform. Amos Rusie won 234 games for the team in the 1890s. Tim Lincecum won two Cy Young Awards. The best pitchers receive it.

In 1951, Willie Mays joined the Giants. His big hits and amazing catches in center field made him a star. Outfielder Barry Bonds set a major-league record for **career** home runs.

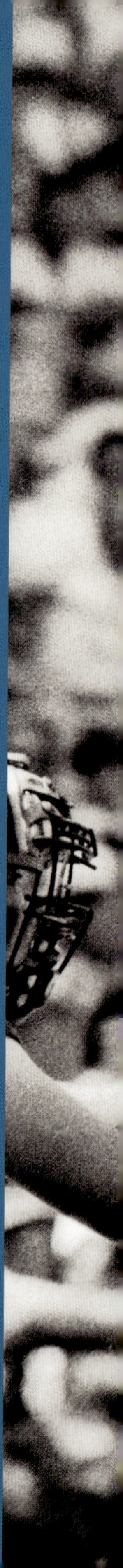

Outfielder Willie Mays

Shortstop Brandon Crawford

Newer players are hungry for more wins. Shortstop Brandon Crawford has earned four Gold Gloves and a Silver Slugger. The best fielders and hitters win these awards. Outfielder Joc Pederson smashed 23 homers in 2022. Pitcher Ross Stripling and fielder Mitch Haniger joined the team in 2023. Fans hope these All-Stars will bring another championship to San Francisco.

About the Giants

Started playing: 1883

League/division: National League, West Division

Team colors: black, orange, and white

Home stadium: Oracle Park

WORLD SERIES CHAMPIONSHIPS:

1905, 4 games to 1 over Philadelphia Athletics

1921, 5 games to 3 over New York Yankees

1922, 4 games to 0 over New York Yankees

1933, 4 games to 1 over Washington Senators

1954, 4 games to 0 over Cleveland Indians

2010, 4 games to 1 over Texas Rangers

2012, 4 games to 0 over Detroit Tigers

2014, 4 games to 3 over Kansas City Royals

San Francisco Giants website:
www.mlb.com/giants

Glossary

career—all the years a person spends doing a certain job

rival—a team that plays extra hard against another team

shutout—a game where one team doesn't score

stadium—a building with tiers of seats for spectators

title—another word for championship

Pitcher Ross Stripling

Index